ACTIVATE

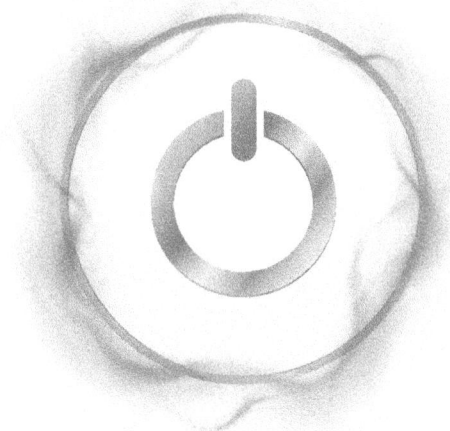

— *Secrets to Living* —
A SUPERCHARGED LIFE

ACTIVATE

Secrets to Living
A SUPERCHARGED LIFE

GENEVIEVE CARVIL-HARRIS

GENEVIEVE

Editor: Adrienne Michelle Horn

Cover Design: I A.M. Editing, Ink

ISBN 978-0-578-54658-2

Printed in the United States of America.

I dedicate this book to every individual who has ever wondered why they never seemed to be able to UNLOCK their vision of success in life. I dedicate this book to those that have packed on years of negative processing because of insecurities, past hurts, and underappreciated self-worth. It is my desire that you would allow this book to help you create space for you to SEE your life differently. You are a WINNER. You just need to be ACTIVATED. I dedicate this book to YOU.

TABLE OF CONTENTS

INTRODUCTION

Let's be clear. You bought this book for a reason. Guess what? I wrote this book for a reason. I want to save people time, and I want to help them with accountability; because we all know that time is money, and nobody wants to waste any of that. If you are anything like me, you do not like to feel stuck or confined too long. This feeling can have a suffocating effect on your vision for the future and can often manifest as stagnation if not shaken.

Have you ever received a gift card? Maybe it was for your birthday or to celebrate an accomplishment, such as graduation. The person who purchased the gift card for you determined the value that it would have prior to you ever receiving it. That card could be worth one million dollars, but you would never have access to any of that money unless you activated the card. The same can be said about life. Each one of us has a purpose and a value assigned to us. However, in order to access the things that we were created to have, we must be ACTIVATED.

Judging by the fact that you are reading these words, you have decided to discover ways to activate your life by identifying the steps that it takes to unlock your vision of success. According to the Merriam-Webster Dictionary, the word "success" is defined as a favorable or desired outcome or the attainment of wealth, favor, or eminence. I am by no credential an accountant or wealth specialist, and therefore, I make no claims to offer great amounts of success or a potential awakening cure. The pages that you will read will be of my own opinion and ideologies that have been formed from life experiences and observations as a capacity-building strategist. However, I do believe that adopting the practices outlined in this book will produce a real change in your life.

WHO THIS BOOK IS FOR?

The "secret" to achieving success in life is one of the hottest topics in America these days. With news indicating that the majority of Americans are in over their heads in debt and rarely have a plan of action to live better, who can blame people for talking about it? Talking is fine. However, there must be some action immediately following if changes are going to be made.

SPOILER ALERT:

THERE ISN'T A SECRET THAT YOU HAVEN'T HEARD BEFORE, JUST STRATEGY THAT YOU HAVEN'T EXECUTED YET.

This book is for those who know that they can't talk their way to the bank. They know that they need a strategy to make a real impact on their future. Too often, we will deceive ourselves into believing that as long as we talk about making more money or achieving success in our lives that it will happen. Some believe that they will accumulate wealth naturally the moment that they cut up all of the credit cards in their homes. We even convince ourselves that we may be able to make up enough excuses to remain mediocre if we don't "measure up" to others. People can even settle to be classified as the "poor" one in the bunch supposing it can't possibly hurt anyone, right? WRONG!

The aforementioned methodologies, all except for the last extreme examples of ineffective thinking, will only work if proper actions are followed to ensure that what has been spoken will actually happen. For example, if I am hungry and I call every living soul in my phone directory to talk to them about my hunger, I would be no closer to actually eating than I was before I made the first call. My hunger would only be satiated once I discover a way to be fed, whether it means that I must purchase food or prepare a meal in the comfort of my own home. In either case, action would need to be taken. This book is for those ready for ACTION.

Who this book is not for?

This book is not for someone that wants a *"get rich quick plan."* It is not for those who want something for nothing. Success is the product of hard work and determination in the right direction. This book is not for those who do not want to be decision makers. Action is what we will be focusing on in this book, as it is what is needed to accomplish any goal. Work with me through this book as we look over the invisible blocks that can easily lead to visible problems that contribute to a lack of success, in some cases, if not dealt with. We will discover the process of having a life that is SUPERCHARGED with value, purpose, and fulfillment. I welcome you on this journey with me to self-discovery and activation of the life you were created to live.

Try not to become a man of success,
but rather try to become a man of VALUE.

-*Albert Einstein*

CHAPTER 1

Discover Your Value

The first secret to having a supercharged life is discovering your value. I heard a story once, while in college, about a little girl and her prized pearl-like beaded necklace. The story expounds by illustrating the young girl's admiration for the value she associated with the beaded necklace. She spent a great deal of her time with it, just as anyone does with something they value. She wore the pearls EVERYWHERE! To school, to church, to sleep, and even when she took her baths despite the green ring they left around her neck. She loved her beaded necklace, and nothing could separate her from them. Nothing had ever tried to. That is until her father asked her to give them to him. "No, Daddy, I love my necklace," she would respond each time her father asked. But he wouldn't stop asking.

Each evening he would lean over as he tucked her into bed and ask for the necklace, but each time she refused. One day the father pleaded with her to just believe that he would not take the pearls away to hurt her. It was then that the young girl decided that even though she loved the necklace, her father loved her much more. If she could trust anyone with her treasured pearl necklace, it was him. The father was so excited to have finally received the necklace. As soon as he tucked it away for safekeeping, he quickly reached for a long velvet box and handed it to her. The young girl was so amazed to find a string of REAL pearls waiting for her on the inside. She had an authentic set of pearls, and they belonged to her. She knew that these pearls must have cost her father a fortune, so she asked, "Daddy, why did you get me this?" His response is the essence of this chapter. He simply replied, "You are worth more than what you loss."

In today's time, it is hard to see the true value of something at first glance. Media outlets promote having a life of perfection, which includes extravagant houses, a forever summer-ready body, conflict-free living, and many other things that the world considers valuable. The ideals of perfect living do nothing more than put individuals in the perfect position to fail. This is because it is easier to go after popular things even if they aren't what you really should be pursuing. This often leads to failed marriages, feelings of depression and low self-worth, and an unrealistic vision for what life is supposed to be.

Much like the young lady in the story, we hold on to things that: 1) Add no value to our lives despite the value we place on them, 2) Eat up way too much of our time without producing worthy results and 3) Leave us with unattractive marks on our lives, even if only temporary. We must understand that it is in our best interest to lose these things or we will find that we have been swallowed up by the "potential" of a situation having ignored the "reality" of it.

LET GO OF THINGS THAT ADD NO VALUE TO YOUR LIFE.

Remember the example of the gift card in the introduction of this book? Let's revisit the emotions associated with that exchange. Somewhere on the card the value will be displayed, and if the truth be told, most individuals respond to the cards based on how much they are worth. A $20 gift card may be tossed around a lot easier than a $2,000 gift card, even though both have a treasured value.

In the story, we saw that the young lady loved the pearl-like beaded necklace that she had. The story did not identify the source of this necklace. It could have been a gift from a local dollar store, or she could have found it outside on the sidewalk. There is no way for us to know where she got this necklace from, but what we do know is that she valued it. Think about the things that you value in your life. Do others place the same amount of value on these items? Do you find yourself justifying your assignment of value to things like your love relationship or close friends to others?

The practice of assigning value to things is troubling because we tend to assign value to everything in life and never really focus on discovering our own value. We have to breakdown the issue that the ideas of value and price have created. Sometimes the mindset that we have been taught growing up is that price and value are equivalent. Therefore, if someone offers a lower price than what is expected, then it can cause someone to question how much it is truly worth. This is evident when people change the price of their products and services to match what they believe others think those products and services are worth.

The general focus of this chapter is to ensure that you know your value. You must know what you're worth! If we do not understand that we must assign value to items that correlate with the prices that we set and then understand where those prices come from, we risk discounting our entire future.

For example, a person could know that a new business project could cost $25,000. If that person starts to believe that the amount seems like an unattainable goal, they may say, "Well, let me start working off of something more realistic." We all have experienced that at one point in our lives, but it's ultimately how you respond to that emotion that makes the difference.

When you are trying to live a supercharged life, it is going to be very challenging for you if words like "realistic" are used to describe your dreams. Ideals and aspirations usually don't ever sound realistic at all. As a matter of fact, most individuals will think that you are crazy for even believing that your life, future, and dreams are worth what you are asking for. Please hear me carefully. That is ok! Just think about how bad you would feel producing something for less that you now have to work twice as hard for all because you did not gather enough resources for it to be successful. Doubting the value that you truly possess inside will cause you to sell yourself short, which would inevitably lead to the world never benefiting from your full potential.

Do not rob yourself of resources, blessings, and connections that you could have gotten because you convinced yourself that your vision, goal, or purpose is worth much less than it actually is. You cannot be upset if someone receives more out of life because they were willing to believe in their capacity to succeed.

What is your activation code?

Now that we have addressed matters that involve price and value, we can now move on to the one thing that grants you access to the value on your card, also known as your life. It's something that you must protect for the rest of your life once you discover it. Your activation code. This code is the key to unlocking the potential of the card. It is the number that is asked for before the representative can grant access to the account. The good news is that everyone has a code. Someone should leap in excitement at the thought of that. You are a winner, and it is about time that you started to act like it. However, there is bad news, too. Yes, I know you weren't expecting me to have any after that little pep talk. But, unfortunately, most people will never discover what that code is.

I do have more good news, though, and this is what changes lives. Someone once told me that the two most important days in your life are when you are born, and the day you figure out why. Although most activation codes vary in length, most consist of eight characters. Funny enough, a date is usually eight characters when reported. For example, 10112014 can easily be read as October 11, 2014. When you finish reading this book, I anticipate that you will begin a journey to discover this code. It will be the day that you discover the purpose of your card. Are you ready to activate your life now? I figured that you would be.

How do you discover your purpose?

Everything that was ever created in this life has a purpose. That purpose dictates the actions of the creation and also how others relate and connect to that creation. Ask yourself these questions and think about your answers. What is the purpose of a table? A car? A garbage disposal? If you are anything like me, you probably visualized how you interact with the objects mentioned above. How did you know what their purposes were? Did the table speak to you and invite you to eat Sunday dinner, or were you taught of its purpose?

Each of us has a purpose, and if you are not taught properly how to discover it, you are setting yourself up for a life of abuse. It has been said that when the purpose of something has not been established, abuse is inevitable. This simply means that if you do not know what something is or what it should be used for, you are likely to misuse it.

Growing up, one of my favorite enchanted movies was about a curious mermaid that would spend her time hoping to be everything except what she was originally created to be. In this quest for transformation, she would find what she deemed to be treasures from another world. What we know to be eating utensils, she would use as grooming tools.

She did not know what it was, nor was she taught. Even her trusted counselors guided her incorrectly.

As a result, this intelligent and inquisitive young woman would create a role for her treasures that did not line up with their true purpose. She was unintentionally abusing the things she believed to be treasures. So many people can admit to being in this exact place in their lives.

You must start to use your innate GPS to get through this life successfully. Let's revisit that thought because your purpose is tied to your personal GPS along with all of your gifts, passions, and skills. You don't have to work very hard at accomplishing these things because you're a natural. I will dare to tell you that you were born to do it. There are people in this world depending on you to be the best you can be so that they can become who they are intended to be.

Of all the things that we are taught in school, somehow, understanding why you were created in the first place never seems to come up. Instead, we are fed career paths based on what our families or communities believe that we should be.

We are told to focus on obtaining an education that will help us become that grand doctor or lawyer, but what about who we were created to be? It doesn't matter how much I dress up my dog to look like a lion or train it to be a lion; he will never be a lion because he was created to be a dog. You can imagine how frustrating it would be for me to try to change my dog into a lion. Yet that is what many parents do to their children. They suffocate the dreams and aspirations of their children because they, too, have been suffocated.

The truth is that the word educate comes from the Latin word *ducere*, which means to draw or to lead. The prefix of the word, which is "e," means out of. Therefore, to *educate* is to lead or draw out of something. This is why so many people go to school for one thing and then realize "I always wanted to be a (you fill the blank)."

I wish to educate you with this book. The purpose of this book is to cause you to seek that which is within and bring it to the forefront of your life so that you can stop wasting your time with dead weight and start living the life you were created to have in the first place. It is my desire that we will be led out of a place of ignorance and into a place of purpose, discovery, and love for who you truly are.

The following are ways to clearly understand your purpose, vision, and goals:

1. Think about your childhood. How did you choose to spend your free time? My makeup artist has been doing makeup since age 14. It was a fun activity for him that no one trained him to do.

2. Identify what activity brings you the most joy. This activity is one that you would still perform wholeheartedly even if you NEVER received payment for it.

3. Find the root cause of the joy that the activity brings you. For example, maybe the reason you find great joy in watching children at daycare is that you truly have a love for the development of children.

4. Find a cause that bothers you and determine what you could do to fix or bring awareness to it.

5. Think of how you want to spend the rest of your life. Where do you see yourself next year? In 3 years? In 5 years? What are you doing in your dreams?

6. If you had a chance to get one million dollars based on the vision and goals you have for your life, what would you present?

7. Are your life goals SMART? That is are they Specific, Measurable, Attainable, Relevant, and Time Sensitive.

8. Discover what people seek you out for most often. Do people come to you for counseling? Do they ask you to do their hair? Do they ask you to speak at their functions? Remember, most often, your natural abilities are tied to your life's purpose.

These are just a few things to help you make your purpose, vision, and goals REAL to you. You were created on purpose with purpose, and it's about time that you realize what that is.

My motto in life is 'Take Risks;'
you don't have a voice if you don't.

-*Kelly Wearstler*

CHAPTER 2

ACTIVATE YOUR VOICE

We are making some real progress already, and I'm proud of you for sticking with it. You clearly want change in your life, and I applaud your commitment. We are just getting started and have some more work to do, so let's dig in.

You know, I was thinking while writing this book that sometimes we go through very difficult times just so that we can learn a lesson, but most times we don't want to go through those difficult times. We say, "Can't life just teach me a better way? Why does it seem like every time we need to learn the lesson it comes so traumatically?"

As a capacity-building strategist, I help people identify where they are and then create a plan with actionable steps so that they can move forward and live their best lives. I can always tell if an individual has suffered from being able to hear and project their "voice" based on how they live. Using this key, it is my hope that others who have "lost their voices" will begin to hear them again.

Growing up, I was always told that silence is golden. I would have to always think about how I was being heard, or how was I being interpreted. People would say things like, "Oh, you just need to be quiet." Since I've always had a big mouth, it's always been hard for me to whisper. But as I got older, I knew what they were trying to articulate to me was that sometimes it's better if people can't hear you.

The problem with that is that we start to learn that our voices don't matter. And that is precisely what I want to address in this chapter. At the end of this written activation call, I want us to understand that our voice does matter. When you have people who are telling you that silence is golden, you start questioning whether it even makes sense for you to articulate things that you may see or hear. It often ends up being thrown into the "maybe I should just keep all of this inside" category of life, and that doesn't help anyone.

What happens next is extremely dangerous. We start to prioritize other people's voices because we've diminished our own. It becomes dangerous for our businesses, our dreams, our families, and our lives. If everybody else's voice becomes so important to you that you don't have your voice anymore, technically, you are left to live by the word of everyone else. Living your life based on the beliefs of others will hinder you from being able to discern what you're doing for yourself versus what you're doing for other people.

As a child, I loved Disney movies, especially *The Little Mermaid* (just in case you didn't catch the clue before). There was a mermaid princess named Ariel, and because she was the princess, we know that we will be following her story. Since she was a mermaid, she naturally had to live her entire life under the sea.

One day Ariel decided that she wanted to be part of a world much different than the only one she had ever been exposed to. She wanted a whole new experience. She wanted to be able to do things like the people she could SEE. So, she started to make up this whole new life that she could have for herself. But we all know that it couldn't be that simple, right?

In order to get this new experience, she had to go to the villain of the story, Ursula, and make a bargain for her new life. Ariel had to be willing to give up her voice - and she does just that. She exchanges her voice for the opportunity to experience what she thinks she wants. Coincidently, this is what I'm finding with individuals in modern times.

We are walking around giving up our voice for what we think we want. During the duration of the movie, the character tries to get what it is that she wants with no voice. She has to make the same steps as everybody else. She has to do what everybody else is doing, but she has no voice.

Instead of enjoying this new experience, she is burdened with trying to find out how she can reclaim her voice. I think that some of us are struggling with that at this very moment. We say, "Oh my gosh, I've given up the things that make me happy so that I can get what I think I want, and now I'm in a place where I don't even like my job. I don't even like what I'm doing, and I've lost my own voice. I don't know what it is that I want anymore, and if someone asked me my name, I wouldn't be able to tell them."

When someone asks you what you want to do, you don't know what to say. You don't know how to say it. You're lost because you have lost your voice. Today I say to you, "Let's get it together." We don't have to continue to stay in a voiceless place. We can make a decision today that declares that "I am going to recapture my voice."

We need to figure out how to hear again, and even more than that, we need to figure out how to speak again. This is because one of the things that we are taught as we grow up is that after you just keep being told, "No, you can't speak. Stay in a child's place," it's hard to start speaking again. I remember it being so hard for me to transition from the little kids' table to the big kids' table or the adult table because for so long I was on the outskirts of life. Everybody was able to speak their minds, and I didn't have the privilege to have an opinion because I was a child. You think that you don't have anything to input. You think that you don't have anything to say or contribute. Then one day you wake up, and all of a sudden, you're grown. And because you're grown, you're expected to have all of these answers. But how? You were never able to engage in the process that would have given you a voice in the first place. So now everyone looks at you as if you don't have a clue as to what's going on, and you're like, "Hey, I haven't been able to speak in all of this time! I don't even know what to do when people are actually listening to me."

So right now, I pose this question to you: What is it that you are giving up your voice for? That's a personal question. One that you don't have to answer today. One that you don't have to answer to me ever. But, you need to start thinking about that. What have you given up your voice for, and is it really what you want? Because in our lives we must get to a point where we start living for ourselves and what we actually want.

As I started helping young people, I found that sometimes they'll go to college because Mommy or Daddy or somebody else wants them to be a doctor, wants them to be a lawyer, wants them to be successful. They find themselves hearing their own voice in their minds, but they're trying to find it because they've lost it.

They often say, "I don't know if what I'm doing is because I actually want to do it or because I think it's what I need to do" or "My parents are going to be proud of me because I think this or because I think that." They've lost their own voice by becoming entangled in who their family thought was going to be the best spouse for them to marry or what their families thought was going to be the best job for them to pursue. Sometimes we allow our enemies to have a bigger voice than we have in our own lives. We will say things like, "I'm trying to do this because I have to show them that they are wrong about me." Saying things like that proves that you are listening to a voice that is not your own.

I want us to get back to a place where we hear our own voice again and allow space to hear the voice of the Lord as well. Sometimes we don't allow ourselves to hear God's voice because we're so caught up in trying to find our own voice. All we hear is the negativity, disappointment, and failed expectations. I'm telling you right now that you must find your voice because if you don't, you will be consumed by the voices of others. You will find yourself disappointed because you will have met everybody's expectations for your life except your own.

With none of your goals met, you feel empty, and you feel alone, and you are left trying to figure out how you've accomplished so much and yet still have nothing to show for it. I used to have nothing because my own voice was hiding and my visions were sitting in a corner, parched with thirst because I had been quenching everybody else's and neglecting my own.

We have to drown out the chatter that doesn't matter. We have to be able to say, "You know, in this season, I just need silence. I need silence from you all because today, I'm making a commitment that my voice is actually going to matter." Now you may ask, "Well, how do you find your voice?" I have more great news for you! I have a solution for you! I am not just writing this book to show you where the problems are but also to provide actual solutions. If I did nothing to help you resolve the problems, then I would only be adding to them.

First, if you're trying to discern whether or not you have lost your voice, write down the last five decisions that you've made in your life. Then write down who helped guide each decision. Whose voice were you listening to for the last five decisions that you've made and was your voice a part of it? Don't think solely about your good decisions. Include the bad ones, too. When people tell us to reflect, we always go straight to the good things, but if your life was that good, you wouldn't need to reflect on anything.

Maybe you have decided to go back to school or to do absolutely nothing. Was that the voice that says, "I want to live my best life" or "I want to be able to have a wealth that can be passed down through generations?" What are you listening to? We need to regulate what we allow to come through our ear and eye gates because those are the things that eventually end up in our minds. We become what we think about, and so we must be careful whose voice we listen to.

Find your voice so that you can live again. Find your voice so that you can win again. When you are trying to find your voice, you need to discover what it is that you want. It may not make sense to anybody else, but when all of the popular social media platforms were getting started, it didn't make sense to everybody. It only made sense to about four or five people. The owners had to make the tough decision to listen to their own voices.

If we investigate people like Oprah, Tyler Perry, and others who are making waves in their communities and the world around us, we will find that at some point, they had to find their own voice. If it meant that they were homeless, if it meant that people didn't support them, if it meant whatever it meant, they got to a point where they decided that their voice mattered and that they were going to speak until somebody listened to them. Even in the Bible, Jesus had twelve disciples following Him. His voice mattered to them. There were a lot more "haters," but his voice mattered to the people who were closest to him. Let us find our voice again so that we avoid repeating what was said before. You have something to say. You have something to add. We have to find that thing. Sit in the room for 15 minutes doing absolutely nothing, except figuring out what you want to do for YOU!

Once you do that, you have a wheel. Something that you're working towards will start to roll. And it will roll because of you and your voice. And let me tell you something, it's so much easier to listen to the voice of God once you get all those negative, crazy thoughts out. When your thoughts are clear, you can easily tell the difference between your voice and God's voice. It is important that we narrow it down to those two voices.

Give no room to the negative thoughts of fear, doubt, and insecurity. Don't think that no one is going to listen to you. I know you have that great project inside of you that only you can share with the world. Speak! So many people are waiting to hear what you have to say.

Stop being silent. UNMUTE yourself. Don't know how to do so? Don't worry. I am unmuting you right now. You are unmuted today! I want to hear what you have to say. The world needs to hear what you have to say. Don't lose your voice. Don't lose your voice for something that you think that you want. It's about moving forward with your voice and knowing that your voice is your power.

Your voice is your power. Speak up. Do not hold your peace in this season.

If you're having trouble finding your voice, there is help. If you've had it and lost it, that's okay. You can lose your voice one day and work to get it back, but don't think that it is going to happen overnight. It won't. But if you just start, you'll find yourself headed in the right direction.

One thing that was so hard for me when I started speaking publicly was listening to my voice. I always had something critical to say like, "Oh my goodness, I sound like that? I really want to sound like this instead." We need to hear our voices again. We need to hear what we are projecting to the world. It will help you determine how much you're worth and how much people should pay you. Sometimes we get comfortable, and we just accept what people give us because their voice matters more than our own. Not anymore. Your voice matters in this season.

If you run into someone who cannot appreciate your voice, you need to remove that person from your life because you are about to get on the megaphone of the century to ensure your voice is heard. When you see my life now, I need you to know that it's because my voice matters to me now. For so long, we have allowed people and their voices to dictate our future as well as what we do. I'm simply encouraging you to make your voice matter. You matter.

We are so quick to listen to everyone and everything that's not connected with our destiny and our purpose. So often we want advice from people who don't even know where they're going. Hello, somebody! I have mentors, and I love my mentors so much. You must be sure that you know what voices to listen to. Sometimes somebody can be your mentor and lead you in the opposite direction of your destiny simply because they don't have the vision to see it. Sometimes the fear of others will be projected on you. Do not let individuals project their fears on you, because pleasing them will only cause you to forfeit your dreams.

Mentors are primarily responsible for planting a seed in you; however, if your mentors are afraid to let you "pass" them, then they may not be mentors at all. We should be able to stand on the shoulders of those who came before us, honor them, and do great works. Please understand, your real responsibility is to do more than those who came before you. Work towards being able to identify your voice so you can know what God is trying to share with the world through you.

I want to close out this chapter by congratulating everyone who is moving in this new season with a renewed voice. I don't do paid endorsements. I only support people who I choose to support. If I have never purchased something from an individual, I won't use my platforms to endorse it. Everybody seems to want a free endorsement these days. I don't want free things because I do not want people to expect free things from me. So, I just want to give a shout out to those of you who have already begun to discover your voice and are going as far as you possibly can. I know things will continue to go better for you as you move forward.

We will find our voices together and start a success choir. All of the voices will go higher, just like the measures of success that we will reach. I encourage you to find your voice in this season. Everybody will listen to what you have to say. Stop telling yourself that no one will listen to you. They will listen once you have found your voice.

When working to activate your voice, I believe that it is helpful to do the following:

1. Reflect on what you have or are giving up your voice for.

2. Write down the last five decisions that you've made in your life.

3. Write down who helped guide each decision that you listed in #2. If you find that your name is nowhere in this answer, you may need to evaluate why your voice has been silenced in your decision-making process. Activate your own voice and begin to live.

Coming together is a beginning. Keeping together is progress. Working together is success.

-Unknown Author

CHAPTER 3

DESIGNATE YOUR AUTHORIZED USERS

As you continue to go through this journey, you will realize that in order to be a true success, you must have a team. I do not mean a group of people that get paid to affirm whether or not your decisions are right. No, I mean a group of individuals who will actually hold you accountable and help your dreams come alive.

For the benefit of those who do not know me, I think it would be helpful to share with you that I went to law school for a year. I was pursuing a lifelong dream that I had since I was 10 years old. Much like many of us, life slapped me right into reality and taught me that my dream life and my destiny were two different things. I believe that God started leading me in the path of community development, and I am glad that I followed.

Even though I left law school early, I still remember quite a bit of the vocabulary and ideas. Failure to appear is when a defendant does not show up for court. This action usually will end up in a penalty being executed against the individual such as an arrest, for example. I don't really want to talk about court though; I want to talk about showing up for your moment to shine.

Often, we find it so easy to show up for everyone else and then when it's time to show up for ourselves, there's a failure to appear. The cycle goes a little like this: You become the ever-dependable biggest fan of everyone in your immediate circle. You are always one call away when needed and always giving when it's time for a donation. But now it's time for you to show up for yourself, and you hit a wall of guilt and fear. Fear will convince you that you are incapable of doing for yourself what you do for others. Can I drop a nugget right here? If you are going to be successful in business, ministry, and your personal life, you have to show up for yourself.

No one is going to show up for us if we aren't even there to show up for ourselves. Have you ever been planning to go meet somewhere and the person you are supposed to be meeting with suggests that the meeting place be their home? How frustrating would it be to arrive and realize that they aren't even at the house? You would have to sit in the car and wait for them to show up so that you could have access to their home. How many individuals have you left outside of your life simply because you were too busy overthinking your dreams and visions to actually show up and make them your reality?

Are you willing to put in the work and do what it takes to get to that next level? In order to live a supercharged life, we have to show up for ourselves first. When we finally get to that point, our presence will teach others to do the same.

I was speaking to a couple of friends once and realized that I could easily be engaged in a phone conversation from 30 minutes to an hour at a time. However, I spent very little time listening to my own thoughts and focusing on what I wanted for my life. You would be so surprised to see how much success you could achieve by sitting in a room and thinking about the necessary steps and action strategy needed to place your life in the right direction. An activated life is a consistent life, and the first place of consistency should be within your own mind.

Your problem areas could become the platforms used to choose your team if you use the right strategy. Watch for the individuals that enter your life with solutions, not drama. If they are willing to show up for you and match your will to achieve, then they deserve to be a part of your team. If they do not add to your life, then you need to hand them over just like the girl did with her necklace. Talking is fine; however, there must be some action immediately following if changes are going to be made.

When we start executing the team strategy and continue to show up for ourselves, others will be able to see your work and celebrate your success. You are as strong as your weakest team member, and so you must challenge your team to show up for themselves before they attempt to show up for you.

There is nothing worse than watching your hard work be thrown away all because you gave someone the authority to act on your behalf who wasn't truly invested in you. We all understand that if someone is not sharing a vested interest or risk, then it is much easier for important matters to fall through the cracks.

Think about your team. Would you send this group of individuals to the store with your $1,000,000 gift card? If not, then you can already see where I am going with this. Your dreams, your visions, and your LIFE are much more valuable than a tangible gift card, so choose wisely who you share them with.

The world is waiting for you to introduce yourself to it, but you are not always the only one handling your introductions. Check your audience to assess who (outside of your team members) is truly supporting you. Again, it is easy to show up for others, but when it's time for people to show up for you, are they giving you the same support that you are giving them? If you have become an ATM and people are withdrawing from you and never making deposits, you will eventually reach a dry place.

What is funny to me is that people will always want you to show up for them but fail to appear when it is time for them to reciprocate the support. It was even this way in history. Multitudes of people were recorded following Jesus when He was on his way to perform a miracle. When He did a sign or a wonder, there was an entire multitude of witnesses that could say, "Oh yeah, he healed the sick" and "He turned water into wine," but when it came time for the trial, there was nobody to be found. Even his close friends denied him. At the moment He needed to feel secure, when He needed everybody to be around Him, nobody was there. I want to encourage you to designate your authorized users and make sure that they are worthy of the title.

There is a difference between people who are your followers and people who are following you. People who are followers, especially in the age of social media, are those who like your status or posts but rarely support you. Your supporters will go wherever it is that you go to offer their love and show their support. A follower can be a spectator, a hater, or one of your worst enemies.

Your followers want to know where you are. They want to see if you're successful. Sometimes people want to see if you're successful just so they can have something to talk about.

Please also note that support from your authorized users does not mean discounts, and it definitely does not mean that you will work for free. My family is full of entrepreneurs, and I pay them money for their services. I don't ask for free things. As a matter of fact, because I believe in my family, I pay for premium services because I want to show them how much I support them.

We must acknowledge in life that true support will always be matched by sacrifice. If the only time that someone can support me is when it's free, I don't see that as valuing my business. I don't see that you value me. If the only time that you can support me is when a value is taken away from me, what type of supporter are you? Are you a supporter of my downfall? If you don't invest in me, I won't have anything to invest in you.

Do not allow these individuals that continually fail to appear in your life have special roles and responsibilities. If they cannot show up to be a part of the journey, they should not be a part of your celebration. Instead, honor the people who offer assistance and support even in their absence. We have to do a better job of assessing support and valuable team dynamics.

Do not allow people to stand with you in your limelight and all of the glory of your victories when they are always failing to appear. I hope that this helps you. I really hope that this encourages you. I hope that it helps all of us to reevaluate our lives and then stretch our capacity for greatness.

When you make the remarkable decision to be a better person, everyone will not rejoice with you. Beware of the haters, naysayers, and vision delayers. You must protect the prized possessions that you have gained.

WHAT WILL YOU GAIN WHEN YOU LOSE?

I recall seeing a commercial that asked a question so pertinent to this book. The voiceover, "What will you GAIN when you lose?" Although she was referencing the physical, I couldn't help but ask these very important questions: What will you gain once you realize that you have lost the blinders in your life? What will you gain once you realize that you are truly free and no longer subject to the mindsets, attitudes, and people that held you captive for years?

For me, it was my joy, peace, strength, awareness, boldness, and clarity concerning my life and purpose. I even met my husband once all of my blinders were dealt with really and truly. So many people lose out on the best moments of their lives because they are stuck hating what they see in the mirror. I do not want that to be your story. The following exercise is designed to help you see yourself for who you really are.

Mirror, Mirror

(Adapted from Ladies Love Yourself founder,
Angela Davis)

Instructions:

Part I:

Take a mirror (size does not matter) and look at your reflection. Speak all the things that you SEE after you say your name. ***Example***: My name is Genevieve Carvil-Harris, and I see... Once you have identified how you see yourself, write down your findings.

Part II:

Put up the mirror again and introduce yourself to the person you wish to see. ***Example***: Hello Genevieve, my name is Genevieve Carvil-Harris, and I am... (insert everything that you wish to be listed) Once you have stated those things, write them down as well.

You will now compare the two lists and devise a plan to become the second list. After that has been completed, you are now ready to write your personal affirmation statement or creed. This will be a series of positive statements about you and your life that you will read every morning when you wake and every evening before you sleep. This exercise will help you be well on your way to embracing the greatness within you.

More important than the quest for certainty,
is the quest for clarity.

-Francois Gautier

CHAPTER 4

CHECK YOUR STATEMENTS

Clarity matters. Before we started school each year, we had to go to the eye doctor. Usually, we would have to stand in front of a board that had multiple letters and multiple lines. We were then asked to read what we saw in front of our eyes. Oftentimes the practitioners would ask us, "Is it clearer in lens one, or is it clearer in lens two?" They would then adjust the focus and ask, "How about now? Is one clear or two?" Sometimes they would even offer a third option. They would do this to demonstrate that no matter how slight the adjustment seemed, clarity matters. We must understand the importance of presenting a clear image in front of others.

When my parents were raising me, they would often ask, "Do I make myself clear?" after giving me a message that they wanted to make sure I understood. And surely, I would say, "Yes, ma'am" or "Yes, sir" to let them know that I understood what they had just shared with me. Any time that question was raised, I knew that they meant business.

When we are thinking about success, we have to understand that we must have a clear picture of what success means to us. Sometimes we set out on the journey to achieving success, without knowing what we should expect as the end result. We have to be clear about what success is to us. Our success is not the same as our neighbor's success, and we must know that our goals will not be the same as their goals either. Whatever it is that you set out to accomplish, you have to be willing to put forth the work to actually make it happen.

First, you should ask yourself if your image is clear? You say you want to be a successful person now that you believe that you know the definition of your personal success, but are you willing to make your image clear? Sometimes there are conflicts between the images we present in our lives and our actual businesses. We say that we want to be successful, but we don't dress the part. Since we don't look the part, people tend not to interact with us. They opt not to listen to our voices regardless of how many great things we must share with the world.

Can you imagine someone dressed in jeans and a polo telling you that he or she was going to a wedding? If that was the dress code for the wedding, we wouldn't judge. However, if that was not the dress code, you would question if that individual was truly going to a wedding.

We have to make sure that the image we present about our future aligns with what we say and the direction that we declared on our lives. Sometimes people use social media to paint a life story that is vastly different than their reality. You browse their page and see things that infer that all is well when that is really so far from the truth. I know individuals on a personal level who will invest hundreds, if not thousands, of dollars trying to impress others with material things and struggle every other day of the week just to make ends meet. If you want to be taken seriously and unlock your vision of success, you first need to be clear about who you are and where you currently are.

That brings us to the second part of this lens of clarity. Is your message clear? Can people understand why they need what you represent? Sometimes people don't or won't support you simply because they do not know or are very confused about what it is that you are promising them. Maybe you're asking them to support the music they don't want to support. You have to make sure that people clearly understand the basis of your message. We are meant to create and sell outcomes and transformations; we do not just sell products and potions.

People invest in what they believe the outcome is going to be. If the sole purpose of the album you are releasing is to help people relax after a long, hard day, then that is what they're really buying. They really are not concerned with how well your beats blend and how nice your voice sounds. After a long day, they will want to achieve a certain result based on your message.

If you are selling a product that's going to help your client base lose weight, then they don't really care about the taste of the product more than the outcome. If you don't have a clear message, people will not buy into your success. Be clear about the desired outcomes for your clients, workers, and program participants. Are you clear about what you are presenting? Make your image clear, make your message clear, and last, but not least, make your success rate clear.

Oftentimes, people want to provide solutions that they have not yet exhausted for their own lives. Is your success rate clear? Do you have any testimonials proving that your methods actually work? That the product you're asking others to invest in actually works? Trust and proof are key. It doesn't matter how many times you say you are right. If you can't prove that what you claim has worked for anybody else, your message will be unclear because your success is not clear.

You will find that more people will be likely to listen to what you say about your life or your business once you can show them that you've made sacrifices in your own life that can be transferable to them. If they can't see you winning, then they will not believe that they can win. They will find someone else who is a winner and follow their methods instead.

If your image, your message, and your success rate are clear, there is no reason why people wouldn't follow you. They would be excited to reap the same benefits you have in your business and in your life. Making yourself clear starts with you! If you are trying to unlock the vision of success for your life, you must make sure that you are crystal clear about your intentions as well as your process. My mom and dad would ask me about whether or not I understood what they were saying, and after I confirmed that I did, I would be able to carry out their instructions because I understood what they were saying. If you want others to follow you and invest in you, make sure that you are crystal clear to others.

Change your M.A.P.

Traveling has always been an enjoyable experience for me, primarily because you start in one place and end in another. Changing locations has always excited me because I've never wanted to be stagnant. My family would go on trips every year, often to places we had not been to the year before, as a means of exposing my siblings and me to places outside of our comfort zone. The only familiar component about our yearly trips was the fact that we knew we would be going to an amusement park.

Amusement parks, for those who have never gone to one, can seem like one huge maze. So, as soon as you walk into the amusement park, there is a station where you can pick up a large piece of paper that outlines every attraction and the food stations surrounding them. As a child, I knew that this map was created to guide me through the park so that if ever I got lost, I would always know how to find my way back to where I should have been.

Each person needs a map or guide to show them where they are standing in life. There are three components to your map that need to be examined to determine if you are on the right path. For the purposes of this book, I will present each component by isolating each letter in the word *MAP*.

M IS FOR MINDSET

The term *mindset* is defined as a set of thoughts that affect one's approach to a situation. In layman's terms, your mindset is the thinking that you have before you attempt to do something. I always say that life can be an exciting journey that you can pack and plan for. However, you cannot predict the weather. The weather can alter what otherwise would have been a perfect trip. For some, the mere probability of rain will alter the way they approach a trip, and that is not good at all. Your mindset cannot be negative if you have any chance of leading a successful life.

Many people never reach past their current positions because their approach is completely off. It has been said that some people are so negative that you have to leave them in the dark to develop. No one wants to be around an individual that is negative all of the time, so it comes as no surprise that those same dark individuals tend to find themselves lonely and stagnant. People that want to be successful speak positive things about their journeys and the steps that they are prepared to take to make it to their destinations in a timely manner.

How many dreams have you let die simply because you did not believe in yourself enough to start? How many opportunities have you let slip away because you approached the opportunity with negative thinking like "They will never choose me" or "I'm not qualified enough?" Approach is everything because without it, you have lost the battle way before there could even be a war. In order to stop this forfeiture from happening, you can do the following:

Think positive thoughts about your current situation and find real answers to any problems you foresee.

1. Write an affirmation statement for your life journey and set goals that mean something to you in order to increase your chances of sticking to that mindset.

2. Do not allow a lack of support or negative speaking to drag you down as you embark on your journey.

3. Changing your mindset means that everything else will change as a result, which leads us to the next letter.

A IS FOR ATTITUDE

Attitude, not to be confused with mindset, is defined as the set of ideas that an individual has that impacts the manner in which they behave. Attitude is the physical manifestation of your unseen thoughts. People near and far should be able to discern how you feel about an issue based solely on your attitude. We can decide that we would like to do something. However, we will come up short every time if our behaviors do not correlate with our verbal communication.

For many years I counseled youth in their transition from high school to college. Each year I would meet a group of students who were excited about going to the college of their choice. Within that group, there would always be a set of students who spoke without any supporting action. They would want to go away for school but wait until the last minute to apply, even after receiving the instructions of how to do it successfully. Our words mean nothing if we are not committed to performing the actions and behaviors to see it through.

The same concept applies to anything. To be successful in life, you must have a successful attitude. You cannot say that you want to lose weight but neglect to make healthy choices. You cannot say that you want to become financially stable and continually practice bad spending habits.

Your attitude is impacted by your thoughts as well as those that you ALLOW to influence you. Some attitudes are passed down through groups of the same socioeconomic status and even the same families. This is why behaviors towards money, education, responsibility, voting, careers, entrepreneurship, family, and a host of other things can be reported similarly in groups of people. This leads us to the final letter in M.A.P., which is people.

P IS FOR PEOPLE

This is such an important area in the clarity of life assessment as many people who lack vision can attribute the blockage of individuals who are in their lives, whether by birth or by self-addition. Blocks can come from the things that have been said by people, done by people, or started by people.

Disclaimer: A person can be classified as a "blocker" in your life and not be a bad person. It may just mean that this person is not adding any value to your life. You must limit the amount or level of interaction that you have with them if you care about your well-being. Ultra-violet rays are not inherently bad. However, if you are exposed to them too long, you can develop very harmful conditions.

People can make or break you, so you must be very careful with whom you allow to be your friends. In addition, you have to be careful with whose opinions your deposit into your life. Friendships are unpredictable relationships in which people have no legal responsibility to each other. Unlike a parent and a child relationship, there is not a natural obligation for friends to do anything for each other. This truth causes one to wonder why so many people allow for individuals with no obligation or authority over their lives to have power over their current circumstances.

Have you ever given someone power over your life? Maybe not knowingly, but your responses days, weeks, and even years after people do things show you who has power over you. Ever thought you were completely over a relationship, and then after seeing the individual for the first time after many years, you couldn't help but admit that you felt something? We give people power in our lives when we give them access to our thoughts and our actions.

Think about your lack of vision in life. How much of it is associated with something someone said to you years ago that stings just as bad today? We have to be honest with ourselves and identify the blocks that have ties to individuals if there is to be any success achieved in unlocking our visions.

USE YOUR G.P.S.

Ok now, not everything is bad. For clarity in your life, we have to check our map. Once we know that it is in place, others can read us much easier. The great news is that you will begin to navigate your way through this journey of life by using your innate God-given GPS system - your **G**ifts, **P**assions, and **S**kills. Everything that you need to survive is already in you; you just have to dig deep enough within yourself to find them.

It is my hope that once you finish this book, you will have access to the winning potential you were born with. I once saw a bird grab a piece of bread and use it as bait to catch a fish out of the pond. I recall thinking to myself, *surely if the Almighty Creator of this universe could equip a bird with the survival skills it needs then we too must have everything we need already as well.* Let's do the work, and let's check our statements!

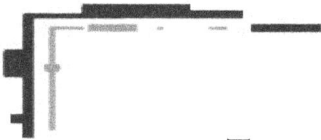

Time and Balance:
The two most difficult things to have control
over, yet they are both the things that we do
control.

-Catherine Pulsifer

CHAPTER 5

Check Your Current Balance

Each one of us has a capacity, and we must identify what we can take. If we don't understand what we can take, we can unknowingly put too much on our plate. When we were younger, our parents or teachers would tell us to eat what was on our plate first before trying to place more food on it. Most times, this was an attempt to test whether our eyes were bigger than our stomach's capacity. In life, we can end up putting so much on our plate simply because we really do not know how much we can actually take on and be successful.

I strive to help individuals understand what their capacity is so that when they start to pile up their plate, they can then make action steps that can take them to the next level. Gratefully, I've been successful and have had the pleasure of witnessing people double their incomes, find purpose in their lives, and go forward.

What does it mean if that relationship isn't there anymore? What does it mean if that friend who was my confidant, isn't there anymore? What do I do?

This job isn't doing anything for me anymore, but I'm still here because what else am I going to do?

If you find that something is no longer functional in your life, you need to reassess what you bring to the table and what everything around you brings to the table. You have to remember to RELOAD. If you can remember to charge your phone after a long day, how much more should you remember to charge your life? Get out of your feelings and step forward into your destiny by being ok with change.

Trees are very interesting to me. If you ever have the time, examine a tree. They come in all shapes and sizes. Some tall and some short, some wide and some thin, some bumpy and some smooth, the list goes on and on. But, you will never find a tree that is rootless. Every living plant, including weeds, has roots and much like our lives, if we can determine the issues at the root, we can diagnose the health of the tree.

We are all trees, each with our own purpose and fruit to bear. We must understand that others depend on our fruit to survive as well as ourselves. So, we must take an active role in ensuring that our trees (lives) are producing the kind of fruit that can make a difference.

Some roots run deep while others are plainly seen. I implore you to check your roots. It is very important to not only identify the root of an issue but also address it.

Oftentimes, as humans, we opt to treat the symptoms and ignore the reality that there is an underlying issue that is causing the problem. We need to make sure that we're not in things just because they are comfortable. We need to let go of our fears and move out of our comfort zones. We cannot hold onto things simply because they remind us of something else.

We have people who are maintaining relationships right now for the memories of how things used to be and then become upset when those same people either can't or won't provide the things they used to. That person was not supposed to be forever. I notice that activated individuals can find themselves completely depleted of all their newfound resources if they do not check their current balance.

It doesn't make much sense to realize that there is greatness in you and then spend all of your precious time pouring that greatness into people and things that can't and won't appreciate it. Nothing lasts forever, so you must preserve your energy for what will truly matter in your life. Know your capacity at the starting point and then make sure that you live a balanced life.

When the toy company built the bear, it was supposed to be used for the lifetime of the battery placed inside of it. Sometimes we want things to be battery operated so that we can prolong their lives by simply exchanging batteries. Mr. Teddy taught me a valuable lesson - life is not that way.

That person was only supposed to be with you for a season. You were only supposed to have that job for that season. I don't have a problem at all with where you start out, but I do have a problem with staying in a place after you have clearly outgrown it. Could you imagine if people were walking around in baby clothes during their adolescent years? We would respond with a series of questions to see why the individual thought that this was acceptable. We would be critical and address the fact that there needs to be a change. However, some of you are still walking around in your "baby clothes" in life knowing you have outgrown them. It is time for a change.

I see this same problem on a number of weight loss blogs. People will hold on to clothes that they cannot wear anymore in hopes that one day they will be able to wear those clothes again. Have we ever considered that maybe when it does not fit anymore, it just may be time to move on? I'm not trying to get back to a place where I fit into things that I used to wear; I want to get new things. Even if my size goes back to that place, I don't want to go back to those clothes. I want new clothes in the new season. I want to see my current, not my past. Although I still have Mr. Teddy, the things that I needed and expected from Mr. Teddy are now obsolete. I no longer expect him to give me comfort.

I submit to you that if you aren't uncomfortable, you aren't growing. And that is what makes changing so hard. It is not supposed to be comfortable. When a caterpillar is in a cocoon, it is struggling. What science tells us is that if you try to help the caterpillar in its cocoon, you can cause deformity and it probably won't be able to fly. Did you know that? When you are in the cocoon of life, and there is a change occurring, it may be hard to transition to the next phase, but I promise it will be worth it.

People may see you in your cocoon and want to try to help you, but don't let them. You have to be able to go through this season on your own because their help may cripple you. This change needs to happen in order for you to walk into your new season.

You can't continue doing your job the same way. You can't keep running your ministry the same way. You can't keep running your business the same way. Check your balance.

You may need to change accountability partners. If there's a new change and that person is not willing to upgrade their life package with you, then they cannot go with you to the next season. We hear it articulated as you have to cut people off, but I'm not sure that I agree. I believe they should be reassigned. Reassign where you have placed them so that you can change their function in your life. Remember to stop giving seasonal things lifetime opportunities in your life.

You were never intended to remain comfortable; you were created to evolve continuously. I'm a really big advocate for evolving into a better person. I believe that you should not stay the same person all of your life. The way that you do things should be evolving just like the way that you approach and conquer your fears should be evolving.

What you do not get to do is criticize somebody for what they have and what they take advantage of simply because you no longer are in that place. That is unacceptable. It's unacceptable to say, "Oh my goodness! I know something better, so now I just get to look down on others." You will never elevate if you only plan to look down on somebody else. Elevation is supposed to put you in a place where you can look down and ask, "How can I build the escalator that is going to help somebody who could not climb up on their own?" When you elevate, help somebody educate themselves so that they can come up to your level as well. Success is best served as a corporate dish.

If you do the work, elevation will be a part of your life, but if you can't sustain it, what's the point? Your elevation makes you a trailblazer with the intent to be an aid to those that come behind you. You are changing in your life so that you can help other people change, but you can't do that from a comfort zone.

I want to see my life differently. I want to see everything change for the better. Sometimes we make changes that aren't for the better. Wouldn't you appreciate it if you could get more clarity about your life and find that the next year of your life is much better than any other year you have ever had?

Decide that enough is enough. This is going to be the last moment where you sit in a place without having what you are supposed to have. This is going to be the last time that you are not connected with your family. This is going to be the last year that I'm not making the salary I want to make. This is going to be the last year that people do not receive what I know I'm supposed to give. Enough is enough.

At what point will you live the life that you're supposed to live? When? Start today. Make the commitment to do whatever you need to do. Break out of your comfort zone and make time to be great. Become a student of life and do not be afraid to learn, re-learn, and unlearn. This will all be beneficial for your journey.

Gandhi said that we must be the change that we want to SEE in this world. I'm encouraging you to be the change that you want to SEE in your life. If you want to give yourself a raise, create a legal stream of income, and change your MAP regarding your finances. The game is meant to be changed. Mark

Zuckerberg changed the game. Oprah changed the game. Tyler Perry changed the game. Sometimes you don't have to play by the rules; you can create your own. Break out of your comfort zone today and change the game altogether.

It's time for a change, and I believe that it is going to be a great change because you're going to be committed to that change. Right? Of course, you are! You have a game to win.

There are no shortcuts to any place WORTH going.

-Beverly Sills

CHAPTER 6

Dᴏɴ'ᴛ Cʜᴇᴀᴛ ᴛʜᴇ Sʏꜱᴛᴇᴍ

Have you ever had a time where you wanted to get into a room that seemed to be locked? I did that often. My parents would lock their doors so that I would not get into their rooms, but I was a clever little girl, and so I would always pick the locks. The problem with picking locks is that you are giving yourself access to an unauthorized level that you did not work for. There was a reason why my parents didn't want me in their rooms. There were possibly things that may have been damaging to me if I had been exposed to them during that part of my childhood. Maybe a picture. Maybe a video. Who knows?

I knew that I was not allowed to be in that room, but I found a way to get in there to get what I wanted. That is how a lot of us behave in life. When locked out of certain channels of life, we may think it is best to pick the locks to get to the next level. The problem is that if you do not work to get to that level, you won't be able to sustain your entry there.

I used to play a video game where if my character had enough diamonds at the end, it would be able to go to the next level. Sometimes I would try to see if his presence in front of the gate would be enough, and it never failed to disappoint me. Every single time I would be sent back to the previous level. I would have to attain every goal set before me if I wanted to open another door. If it seems that doors are locked or roads are blocked in front of your purpose, it could be because you haven't done enough to open those doors. Cheating the system won't help you. Just do the work! Put forth the maximum effort so that access can be handed to you when you have earned it.

I'm reminded of a time when my husband and I went to Jamaica. We had chosen to stay in an all-inclusive resort. It was so beautiful. It appeared to have two sides, so we asked our escort to drive us to the side that we had reserved. Unbeknownst to us, he took us on the VIP side instead.

When we arrived, the hostess gave us all types of beautiful things. We had servants there waiting on us hand and foot. We truly felt like **V**ery **I**mportant **P**eople. Then came the moment of truth. It was time for us to present our credentials to the hospitality staff at the front desk. That is when we realized that we were on the wrong side of the resort. While it was not our fault, we were not supposed to be on that side, so the staff politely directed us back to the side that we actually paid for.

When you are trying to get to a level in life that you haven't done the work for, eventually the day will come where you'll have to present your credentials in order to remain there. If you don't have the correct credentials, you will be sent back to where you should be. A lot of people want VIP treatment with only having to do general admission work. If you haven't done the work, then you need to go back to the drawing board and figure out what plan of action you need to execute so that you can be qualified.

Let's look at the three different types of people that you'd find in a VIP area of life. First, we have those who paid to be in the VIP section. These individuals are those that may _pay_ very high prices to be amongst the people who are in the VIP section. Then there are those that have _done_ enough to have their fees waived because of the value that they bring to the table. Celebrities fall into the third section and usually would not have to pay to be in the VIP section simply because people will pay money to share the same space with them. Even then, people will attempt to sneak past security to be with those that possess value. However, if they don't have the right wristband or credentials, they will be moved back to general admission tickets.

If we are going to unlock this level of success, then we have to understand that respect is earned. If you try to steal it, it won't last long at all. Everyone has to pay their dues. You have to put in the work. You cannot just walk around picking locks and cheating the system.

People desire originals, not imitations. You have something great in you. Your vision is original, so do yourself the favor of actually putting in the work so that the others in the world can get what they're supposed to get from you. We don't get anything out of people that copy someone else's strategy and methods.

Don't be tempted to cheat, especially when your ideas could have produced better outcomes. Take your time. Wait for the key. If you do the work that you're supposed to do, sooner or later somebody's going to call you and offer you a key to unlock the door that has been locked to you. You are a winner, and true champions never have to steal what already belongs to them. Be patient and work.

Take a moment and think about the following things:

1. Identify the true essence of what you desire. If it is a job you desire, what barricades do you have in your way? What will do to make sure that you do not take the easy way out?

2. Understand that success is a process and not just a one-day event. Even if someone looks like they have achieved success overnight, I can guarantee you that you haven't seen the work done behind the scenes.

3. Decide to appreciate and hold on to the things that you currently have. Do not cheat the system by copying others. There is already enough greatness in you to become successful in your own lane.

4. Create a maintenance plan for your newfound appreciation of life.

5. Move forward, connect with others who are likeminded, and do not rehearse the practice of comparing yourself to others around you. Focus on your ability to add value to any room that you walk into.

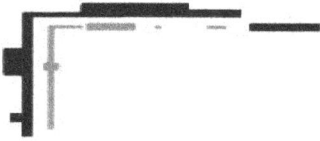

Success is not final, failure is not fatal: it is the courage
to continue that counts.

-*Winston Churchill*

CHAPTER 7

LIVE ABOVE SEE LEVEL

I hope you guys are still awake, charged and ready to continue. We have covered a lot of ground, but there is still more to address. One of the easiest ways to blow through valuable material is to rush and try to do everything at once. Remember, sometimes your eyes are bigger than your stomach. You can pile things so high that you become overwhelmed by what is directly in front of you. You have to be able to see what's beyond your current place in life if you are going to live a supercharged life.

When the storms of life come and box you in, you will only be able to survive if you have purchased non-perishable items with all of the value that you've been given along the way. People will spend valuable time and energy on items, projects, and people that will only stick around for a little while. Living a supercharged life means that you have discovered how to allocate the time and resources needed to sustain you.

To embrace something you love, you usually will have to confront something that you hate. So, let's start there.

One of the most despised words in my vocabulary for the longest time was the "F" word. I mean, as soon as I heard it, I would immediately think, *do you kiss your mother with that mouth?* Yes, you guessed it! FAILURE. What a word. I figured for years that it meant that I was incapable of success, that I did not have what it took to be "somebody." I was to run from that word as far as I could, and I dared not hang with individuals that made it a way of life. The fear of this word paralyzed me for many years, and I was sure that if I failed at anything, I was missing out on life.

I offer to you today that if I had never learned how to handle past failures and those that are to come, I would have ceased to live life as intended. You cannot be truly successful without failure; it is a part of the process. Failure is in success' recipe, so to run from failure is to run from success, and no one knowingly runs from success. Or do they?

Failure is not final. I really want to express this because I am a perfectionist. You can judge me, but confession is good for the soul. I've been a perfectionist since I was a little girl. If I didn't get straight A's in school, I would cry because it meant that I must have done something wrong. For as long as I can remember, perfection was always important to me. Long before perfect eyebrows, make-up blending, and jewelry accessorizing even made the list, my ideals were centered on having a perfect educational record.

According to my parents, school was my job, and it was my responsibility to make sure that my job paid well. In other words, my grades were the keys to getting the things I wanted in life. I would think that I was less than and I didn't know how I was going to be able to make it to the next level if I failed. But you know what happened? I kept on winning.

So, I want you to know a secret. Your failures in life are not fatal. They aren't going to kill you. I know your mind is blown right now, but I have to say it again. Your failures will not kill you. You have to start understanding what failure is. By definition, failure means that you have a lack of success. What is success? Success is when you reach an achievable goal, aim, or purpose.

When someone fails, it means that they did not reach the goal. For example, you may have said, I'm going to lose 10 pounds, and then you lose seven pounds. Instead of rejoicing about the seven pounds, you get upset that you didn't get rid of the other three. You consider this as a fail, and by definition, it is. However, you were able to do something that you didn't do before.

We must learn to rejoice in what did happen and stop beating ourselves up over what didn't. We must get to the point where we change our perspective and say, "You know what? I didn't fail at this. I just didn't make it this time." Then you will be able to figure out what is needed in order to achieve success next time. That is how you become successful in your business, ministry, and personal life.

When you start to understand "I'm not a failure; I just lost seven pounds," then you can plan your next steps and celebrate them by buying some ice cream. Ok, maybe not ice cream, but you get my point. You celebrate the fact that you actually did something. You are not a failure just because you don't reach every single goal. What I find is that I actually think that it makes you more profitable to fail. That promise you make to yourself every year: saving money, exercising more, eating right. You know the drill. Not meeting the goal does not give you the right to lose hope and tell yourself that it will never happen; it just should get you charged up to conquer your next goal.

Look at what you consider to be a past failure and look at what has come from it. A common mistake that we make about life is that if we do everything right, it makes us exempt from hardship. Truthfully, hardship makes us qualified to be winners. Think about it this way. If you went to the doctor for an interview to determine whether or not the doctor could handle being your primary care provider and the doctor told you that all of his or her patients were always healthy and never suffered from any illnesses, would you feel comfortable going to this doctor?

I hope your answer is NO. If a doctor has never seen illness before, how will he respond when you are sick? I would never want to go to a doctor for surgery, and they have never failed. No. I need to know how you responded if somebody died on your table. I don't want to be anybody's first mess up. I need to know your record. If your record shows that you've always won and that you don't know what failure is like, then I don't necessarily know that I want to work with you. I need to know how someone bounces back from failure.

Exposure to things not going quite right actually qualifies people to prescribe assistance. You have to move beyond what you see right now and fight for what you want to see. You should think about that the next time a trial comes your way, and you are faced with failure. Remember you want to understand your failure, not hate it. This is how you gain knowledge, and that is how you ultimately become successful.

Do not hold on to past hurts and failures. Use them to justify your life's stagnation. Pick yourself up, dust off the weight of your past, grab some strength for the future, and move forward.

Sometimes failure is going to happen even after you've done everything right. It's okay. It's a part of the process. I attended law school for a year, and I remember trying my best to do everything right. All of my papers, all of my exams, everything that I had to do, and it never seemed to be enough. That doesn't make you a failure.

Some will quit in the middle of the process because they have failed at something. Sometimes you have to lose so that your strategy can become stronger and your wins can be sustainable. Do not forget the pearls. You give up in life in order to gain, even if it feels like failure at the time.

I don't want to just win one championship. No, I want to be like Steph Curry and Lebron James and learn how to live above SEE level. At one point, Lebron was failing in Cleveland. He would make it to the championship but could not win the ring. He knew he had to be more strategic. He needed to go to a place where he could win. And that place was Miami. I'm a Miami girl, so allow me to shout, "One time for the Miami Heat." He came to Miami, but when he came, it was to learn a system. He came to learn and understand what the team was doing. They all had the same resources - great coaches, a basketball, a team, and jerseys.

What was the difference? The difference was that Miami had a winning system. So as history would have it, he comes to Miami, learns the system, and then is able to go back to Cleveland and win a championship. Lebron James is not a failure. He knew he wasn't a failure, but he was playing into a failing system. I want to challenge you to analyze whether you are playing into a failing system. If so, then that's what makes you feel like you're a loser. It is making you feel like you're a failure, and you are not one.

I want you to change your perspective. Change how you see this. Say, "I am not a failure. I am playing into a failing system, and I need to figure out the tools of the trade so that I can start to learn lessons that will improve my performance." Not a top-shelf secret, but sometimes applying this mindset can change the way you live forever.

Think about the fact that sustainable wins are transferable. When Tyler Perry was first introduced to the world, he was the writer, producer, director, and songwriter. He did everything. That worked for a season in his life, but it worked as long as his vision was small. The moment he started expanding to television and film, he needed to create a system where other people could plug into the system and help him reach his goals more effectively and much quicker. You may have a system, but it may be failing simply because you're the only one operating it. I am consulting you to build the system. Teach people the system and give them purpose by allowing them to work that system. You'll see the great returns because you took the time to break your failures into many strategies that could be duplicated and done over and over again. Do this, and one day you will check your bank account and say, "Oh my gosh, I love Genevieve because she took this big goal of mine and put it into small little steps, and now my bank account is showing me greatness."

Learn from all of your mistakes, no matter how large they may be. Learn from your $10,000 mistakes so that they don't become $100,000 mistakes. You don't have to run away from success because you see failure as an ingredient on the back. You are taught to read all of the labels when you're trying to lose weight and be summer-ready all year long. Well, success has branding too, and on the back of that label, failure is mentioned. If you're allergic to failure, you will never be able to taste success. Don't run from failure, embrace it. Activate your life because hidden in every failure is a greater win. Success is available to you, even though failure may be included in the packaging.

Leaders become great, not because of their
power, but because of their ability to empower
others.

-John Maxwell

CHAPTER 8

Swipe Right

Have you ever been traveling somewhere and not known exactly where you're going? If your friends are anything like mine, someone may volunteer to lead the way. Now that is fine and dandy until they forget that you are behind them. As they are driving, you realize that they start switching lanes much quicker than you can catch them. It could have been a lot easier for you if the person had used their signals to let you know which direction they were moving in. It can be frustrating to follow somebody who doesn't signal you in the right direction. It is even worse if that person is the leader of your business or your ministry.

It is clearly seen when a leader chastises you for not doing something correctly even though you were never trained. That is why I named this chapter Swipe Right. As leaders, friends, and people, we must use our signals properly so that our communication and success flows in the same direction. If we do not swipe our gift cards correctly in the store, then the transactions cannot be processed. If we do not swipe right in life, then the people who are following us are more likely to get lost. A system will not work if everyone on your team gets lost before reaching the destination.

No one is perfect. I know this. Sometimes we don't have all of the answers, but we have to hold ourselves more accountable and know that, if we have people following us, then we are leaders. It does matter whether we asked them to follow us or not; we are held to the same standard.

Some people have the presence of a leader long before anyone gives them a title. Once they start to have the influence of a leader, there is no turning back. It's not about whether or not you ask people to follow you. If people are following you, there's a charge that you have to keep. That's the interesting thing about social media. Remember when we addressed followers? Everybody wants them, but they don't understand that it is going to make them a leader. If people are following you, where are you leading them?

Understand that as a leader, you cannot post everything that you want to post because you may be signaling wrong, or in this case, "swiping left." You can signal people in the wrong way if you project things one way and then live another way. Your followers are not mind readers; they respond based on what you present. If you present wealth on Monday, you cannot present a lack of resources by

Wednesday. This will cause confusion. People will be bound to be misled by the leaders' inconsistency. Be sure that you are familiar with the lane you are driving in before you try to lead someone else in it.

As leaders, our greatest asset is being able to use our own experiences to help others avoid the issues we encountered. We can direct the path because we know the lanes and the exits along the route to success. Sometimes people are so caught up in their own experiences and the fact that no one showed them how to win that they are reluctant to swipe the right way and leave footprints for others to follow.

As a matter of fact, there will be instances where we just need to put on our hazard lights to let individuals know that the right thing to do is not to follow us. You should be equally concerned about their successes and their failures. It is ok to tell our followers to go around when we find ourselves in positions that don't allow us to lead effectively. Let's start using our signals. We use them in our cars, but we need to use them in our lives. It's okay to have signals that say, "I know I'm your leader, but I am human, too. And today, I just don't feel like it." I feel like we would have a lot less confusion if people would just be honest with themselves and others. I am encouraging you to live a supercharged life of optimal success, not an overcharged life that is ineffective.

Sometimes we put ourselves on pedestals, and we let people put us on pedestals and everyone involved forgets that we are still human beings. So, let's just get back to a place where we can recognize and appreciate the humanity of each other so that we're not scared to show our signals. I've personally witnessed people say stuff things like "Nobody checks on me" or "Nobody cares about me." My response is usually to respond by drawing attention to the visible signs that the person is displaying. If every one of your social media posts makes you look happy, excited, or joyful, how in the world would anyone know that they were supposed to cheer you up? You have to swipe right in order for your messages to go through.

We want sacrifices from people, but we're not willing to make them. It should not be this way. We have to be charged up about actually giving people something to follow. You want followers, but you're not giving. You're not paving ways for anyone. How does that make sense? Our signals have to be honest and transparent because if you're not, people will strive and aspire to have a life that doesn't even exist for you.

After a busy ministry and business week, my sister said, "Oh my God, you're superwoman." I said, "I don't aspire to be." I don't aspire to have this supernatural strength that allows me to develop a false identity and put so much on myself that I'm not able to carry my purpose. I don't aspire to do that. What I do aspire to do is to inspire you to be the best version of yourself that you can be so that the world can be a better place because you are living in it.

We need leaders like you. People worry about stepping out and getting charged up because they think that the market of leadership is oversaturated. Listen, you are not less of a leader if the people that follow me don't want to follow you. There is a target market within your industry waiting on you to swipe right and show them the way.

Leadership requires more, and to whom much is given, much is required. We must lead by example. If you're not ready to lead or are equipped to lead, then you should sit down and get trained. Leaders need to be trained. You don't wake up a leader. You may have leadership qualities in you, but the truth of the matter is you should want to be led first so that you will understand how to deal with followers.

There are some things that your leader will never share with you, and it's simply because it's not for the masses. However, if you are training to be a leader, you will find out that some things are taught, and others are caught. The pressure that is put on them to hold up certain values and the standards forces them to conduct themselves differently even when they should not have to.

You cannot effectively lead or manage people if you lack interpersonal skills. Leadership is practiced. Not so much in words but as in attitude and in actions. Sometimes we lead in our silence, in our integrity, and in the way that we do things. John Maxwell states that a leader is one who knows the way, goes the way and shows the way.

Who are you training to carry your torch? If you are carrying the torch and then something happens to where you are no longer able to carry it, that torch is going to hit the ground and set the entire village on fire if you didn't have anyone designated to carry it in your absence.

You have to know the way! You have to go the way!! You have to show the way!!! Everybody needs a leader to hold them accountable, to push them, and to challenge them for more. Can I just be honest? I never liked to hear "what's next?" when speaking to my mentor, but I had to receive that level of questioning. I knew that if I planned on going to the next level in my life, I would have to be open to correcting the level that I was on while investing in levels that activated my destiny.

I encourage you all to use your signals in life. There are people following you, and you have to make sure that what you do, what you say, and what you show will teach them how to manage this next season of life.

What's driving you? Think about that for

a second. If pride is driving you, it will always lead to a dead end. Pride comes before a fall and destruction. If people are following you and you're on your way to being destroyed, they are on their way to destruction as well. So, swipe right like lives depend on it. Truthfully, they really do.

Success has a price that only those that don't
care about the price tag can afford.

-Unknown Author

CHAPTER 9

ACCEPT THE CHARGES

The love of money is said to be the root of all evil. Not getting it, just the love of it. People often mistake the phrase for suggesting that having money is the root of evil, and that is why I wanted to make the distinction early. Everything in life worth something will cost you. So, you need to accept the charges instead of looking for an easy way out. A supercharged life is an expensive one and may cost you long-time friendships and even coveted possessions. You should never really love money or things more than you love helping people. You should embrace the fact that money is a tool, nothing more. Think of it as a hammer. It is something that, when used properly, can help you build systems to introduce generational wealth and financial freedom to your family for years to come.

You don't have all of this vision for nothing. You were led to this book for a reason, and you are still reading it because somewhere in your heart and mind, you know that what you have read is true.

You've been unlocking all of the doors of your mind while reading and your vision is breaking through the surface. It has led you here. This is where we accept the charges in life in order to monetize the future. A wonderful book that I read daily teaches that without vision, the people perish. People perish when they don't have anything to go off of. No model for success. No mentor or guidance. With what you learned in the previous chapter, I know that those around you won't perish because you will give the right signals and directions. People will follow you and no longer be lost.

Someone's life is depending on your vision, and that should come at a cost primarily because your vision wasn't free to you. When you are pursuing your purpose-filled vision, you will have long nights. Maybe even sleepless nights. You will find that you have to sacrifice going to events with your family and friends in the best interest of investing in your future. I don't mean that a supercharged life is boring or lonely. I am simply stating that when you decide to accept the charges that come with it, sacrifices will be necessary. The most successful people in the world have sacrificed to acquire what they want. Success comes at a cost, so why would you give somebody something for free that cost you so much time, money, and effort. You must accept the charges associated with your life so that you don't sell yourself short when it is time to charge others. People will pay great sums of money for things that will change their lives.

You should not ever chase money; just focus on how you can change somebody's life. Even if you don't think that what you do is all that important, I am willing to guarantee you that it means more than you could ever imagine to someone else. Think about it. If you had a class paper to complete and it was worth fifty percent of your final grade, I'm sure that it would probably be pretty important for you to complete it. Let's say that your computer started to experience a glitch and you needed to turn in your paper by a certain time. Stress, anxiety, and fear could easily flood your mind, and there would be no amount of money that would seem unreasonable if it meant that a technician could come and fix your computer.

You would hope and pray that the person can fix your computer in the quickest amount of time possible. The amount of money that you pay would be worth having your problem resolved. Sometimes individuals suffer from the idea of monetizing their visions because they do not even value their own work. No one can do what you do in the same way that you do it. The world needs your expertise, and if you have done your due diligence in service, then no one should question why they must pay for your services. At best, they should ask if you have payment options. Accept the fact that having a supercharged life means that you have to make tough decisions sometimes in order to secure your long-term victories.

One of the hardest things to do in life is to lead yourself. We have already spoken about leading others, but it seems even harder to do when you are trying to lead yourself. Whether it's leading your home in healthy eating or establishing a workout plan, it is hard to lead. This is not because it takes so much out of an individual but rather because that individual has to look inward for a strength that will not only keep them motivated but also motivate others. I used to wonder why so many people were followers of crowds and movements that they did not understand. Most of the time, you have a group of people who lead, and everyone else follows. No one wants the responsibility of leading. This is because most people do not trust themselves to make wise decisions for their own lives.

I had to think about my success in a more practical way to understand why my way of thinking was contributing to my feelings of stagnation. If I want a house built and I have secured the finances to hire individuals to build the house, I would want my money to be well spent. To receive anything other than what I paid for would be utterly unacceptable, and I would be visibly upset. Well, taking that into consideration, if the contractor informs me that he will build my house in forty days without any assistance from anyone else, I would probably question his sanity. I definitely would question the quality of his work along with the longevity of my house. It is safe to say I would not enter into a contract with him. It would be even worse if the contractor suggested that he could achieve success on my house sooner than forty days by using fewer products. However, few people question the promises of success that incorporate the use of mediocre principles or get rich quick schemes. Smart work will always allow you to secure a better future.

I would like to think that your life means more to you than the house mentioned in my clumsy example. If we would question the long term benefit of having a house built in forty days, then why on earth would we believe that our lives which have been filled with poor decision making for years would just snap together into the perfect image of success after a month or so? You can listen to the best coaches in your field or read the best self-help books around, but it doesn't happen overnight.

This can be seen in the lives of others as well as the quest for success. So often we witness family members and friends fall into wanting what others have. I cannot begin to describe the numbers of people that have said to me "I wish I had a spouse like that" or "I wish my life was like this person or that person." I hate to be the bearer of bad news, but if you are not willing to do exactly what that person did to attain their apparent success, then you need not speak of it.

How many failed relationships, untapped potential, and years of stagnation have stemmed from your quest to be like someone else? And for the less transparent reader, how many lives have you seen affected by others running behind a life and destiny other than their own? We all have a purpose, and it does you no good to run after someone else's destiny and live a life full of regrets and "shoulda-coulda-woulda." You can never be another person, no matter how hard you try or how close you get. Imitations are never as good as the originals. You should never sell yourself short by comparing your life to the next person. Most times, the person you are comparing your life to doesn't even want the life they have. Accept the charges for your own life's bill and don't spend precious time comparing your bill to others.

My mother used to always tell me, "Genevieve, ART imitates LIFE." She was telling me that what you see on television, in magazines, or on the movie screen is but a mere reflection of reality and that it is up to you to live your real life. Plenty of movies and dramas show that those who everyone thinks have it all together are really searching for the pieces of their lives, too. The only difference is that they can afford to pay for the make-up artists to hide the dark circles from sleepless nights and even abusive relationships. And that goes for both men and women.

Not accepting the charges of one's life would be things like lowering your standards to secure a relationship, pursuing individuals in committed relationships, burning bridges while climbing your ladder to success, forgetting your family name and heritage, and neglecting your faith unless you enter a rough patch and remember that everyone needs a Savior. There is no one that I know personally who has followed any of the aforementioned trends and had a positive result. The funny thing about trendy things is that their results are temporal unless you continue to do the exact same thing you did to get the results in the first place. It's the reason why you can have a friend invite you to become a part of an initiative that they only joined because of a fast start bonus. We've all been there. Once the initial hype wears off, you can find that individual chasing the next check, never really sticking with what they have already started.

I had an undergraduate professor tell me, "You are on a quest to be successful, but you already are. School did not give it to you. You earned it." I didn't hear a word she said at the time. I had made up in my mind that law school was the way to go because I wanted to pursue law from the time that I was 10 years old. I was going to be the female Johnnie Cochran, and no one could tell me otherwise. I took everything that everyone said to me, including my professor's words, as discouragement. I thought people were just being negative.

After my first year of law school, I had to do a real self-analysis and determine what I was supposed to be doing with my life. Johnnie Cochran was a great inspiration to my life; however, it was not my destiny to be the next Johnny Cochran. He had already lived his life and left a legacy. It was time for me to build my own.

It was only after a true, in-depth, analysis of what my passions in life were that I realized why, although very successful, my life felt empty and miserable. I brought unnecessary pressure into my life trying to be someone else when God had given me the tools to be "ACTIVATED" all along. I became so happy once I realized what my purpose was to fulfill on this earth. I had to be ok with not being the person everyone anticipated I would be. It was the beginning of living my supercharged life. Take it from me, success trends are not what you want to follow.

I purchased a bumper sticker for my car once that said: "Are you following Jesus this closely?" If we would use half of the time that we spend focusing on others' lives to address our own personal vices, then we would accept our charges a lot quicker and achieve success. Do not get me wrong, I am a firm believer of seeking wise counsel to help you along in life. The keyword is "wise." What I am encouraging you not to do is choose a person, even your parents, and try to reinvent their life. Take heed to their counsel and set forth a plan to reach your destiny and leave an everlasting mark on this world. Trends are temporary, legacies live forever. We have to make sure that we are solving somebody's problem. Accept the charges, chase purpose, and the money you seek will overwhelm you.

It is AMAZING how your life changes when you embrace the reality that you are better than the life you've SETTLED for.

-Steve Maraboli

CONCLUSION

Do you think you can do this? I know you can. I can't wait to see what happens once your dreams meet strategy and you get to see what those open doors look like. Now is the time for your cash flow to match the flow of your dreams. You've made it to the end of this book. Congratulations. It's been a great journey, hasn't it? I have enjoyed being here with you, and I think that your eyes are open wider than they were when we started this book. If you can understand the principles taught in this book, then your life will change forever. Hopefully, you'll never see things the same way. It was my intention to expose you to a new way of living life, and I want you to see the current that's designed to flow in your life. Think of yourself as a current, as a stream, like a river that flows. Of course, you flow into a bigger ocean like the rest of the world. However, what you provide can only be given by you, so don't worry about the other streams and currents next to you. What you have contributed is just as important. Everything flows. Water flows, electricity flows, charts flow, blood flows, and guess what? Even cash flows! You need to catch the flow and become a part of it.

This has been a great journey, and I can't wait to see what comes of it. I want to welcome you to a life of unlocked success. You have been given a priceless gift card with an immeasurable amount of potential. It is time to be activated. Feel free to schedule a call with me if you are ready to reach the greatness that you know you were created for. Success is yours because now you can see it and you are ready to work for it. I believe in you, and I know that you will sustain. Your possibilities are limitless, and I can't wait until you write to tell me how great you are.

I refer to my clients as Gamechangers, because that is exactly what they are. We have a code language for our wins, and I want to share it with you now. When we become activated, we begin to catch the flow of life. If any of us make income from a new stream of thought, we refer to that as a #reigncheck. This may be a new partnership, product, or service. We post it on our social media and within our private Facebook group, and the entire community celebrates each other.

Whenever a Gamechanger makes money from the system that they've already created, then we refer to that as a #raincheck. Why rain checks? Well, I know that when people throw money in the air, most people say they make rain. Well, we don't want the money to just be thrown in the air. We actually want the money to hit our bank accounts, and that's always in the form of a check. You are going to be moving towards having #rainchecks and #reignchecks. So why not pursue your supercharged life and have rain/reign checks when you write to me? I want you to tell me what you have done and how unlocking your vision has allowed you to have success as shown by the rain checks in your life.

Please do not just let this be another book that you add to your collection. Apply what you have read here and share the information with others, to encourage them to be activated as well. I wish you all the best in your journey. There is greatness in you, and I can't wait to see you live your "supercharged" life.

ABOUT THE AUTHOR

Genevieve Carvil-Harris is the world's favorite Capacity Building Strategist. She is a thought leader, businesswoman, philanthropist, and speaker who gracefully manages life in and out of ministry. As a passionate community developer, she provides valuable and highly effective growth strategies for individuals and small to medium ministries and businesses on a local, national, and international level. Her weekly live broadcast, "Clarity Call" has been viewed by thousands of people seeking her insight and guidance.

She has actively worked as a voice for individuals with dreams that far exceed their circumstances and current budgets for over 15 years. She specializes in capacity building, and dream development strategies and her unique approach to fundraising and corporate development have made her a sought-after consultant and speaker for non-profits and for-profit companies. She has been able to help clients amass from $250,000 to MILLIONS of dollars through executed strategies. Whether through leadership development or resource development, Genevieve desires to "Create, Train, and Cultivate" others. Genevieve has made it her personal mission to help individuals ACTIVATE their lives, which she defines as a supercharged life full of clarity and purpose. She seeks to help 100 people achieve the status of "multimillionaire" in the next 10 years while building legacies and opening doors of opportunity for generations to come. She currently serves as the CEO of Free To Live Management Services and is the leader of DCLARE & DECREE Community Arts Ministry. She is the proud wife of Brian C.Harris.

For Booking Inquiries:

http://BookGenevieve.as.me/
connect@genevievecarvilharris.com

@gencharris

Genevieve Carvil-Harris

Connect Today!

www.ingramcontent.com/pod-product-compliance
Lightning Source LLC
Chambersburg PA
CBHW021343090426

42742CB00008B/720